Rainy Days

By Jennifer S. Burke

SCHOLASTIC INC.

New York   Toronto   London   Auckland   Sydney
Mexico City   New Delhi   Hong Kong   Buenos Aires

Photo Credits: Cover and all photos by Maura Boruchow

Contributing Editor: Mark Beyer
Book Design: MaryJane Wojciechowski

ISBN 0-516-23869-8

12 11 10 9 8 7 6 5 4 3 2 1   1 2 3 4 5 6/0

Printed in the U.S.A.   10

First Scholastic printing, October 2001

Contents

Today it is raining.

The sky is gray.

Rainy days are not very bright outside.

Even on rainy days, I go outside.

I wear my **raincoat** outside.

I also wear my rubber boots.

The **rain** falls on my coat.

9

I like to reach out my hand and feel the rain.

The raindrops splash against my **palm**.

Rain makes my hand all wet.

In the car, I look out the window.

The raindrops slide down the window.

13

My mom turns on the **wipers**.

They wipe away the rain.

Now she can see clearly.

15

We go shopping at the **mall**.

My mother buys a new **umbrella**.

30% off

17

When we get home, it is still raining.

I like to play with puzzles on rainy days.

19

Sometimes after it rains, the sun comes out.

All the green leaves and bushes are bright.

New Words

mall (**mawl**) an indoor place with many
stores

palm (**polm**) the inside of your hand

rain (**rayn**) water that falls from the sky

rainy (**ray**-nee) when rain falls

raincoat (**rayn**-coht) a plastic or rubber
coat that keeps you dry

umbrella (um-**brel**-luh) a thing held over
your head to cover you from the rain

wipers (**wy**-perz) rubber arms that wipe
away water by moving back and forth

Index

About the Author

Jennifer S. Burke is a teacher and a writer living in New York City. She holds a master's degree in reading education from Queens College, New York.

Reading Consultants

Kris Flynn, Coordinator, Small School District Literacy, The San Diego County Office of Education

Shelly Forys, Certified Reading Recovery Specialist, W.J. Zahnow Elementary School, Waterloo, IL

Peggy McNamara, Professor, Bank Street College of Education, Reading and Literacy Program